LORNA DOONE

R. D. BLACKMORE'S FAMOUS STORY

Simply Retold

By S. E. LATHAM & S. E. WELLER

Illustrated by: Jo Brown

D1513962

QUEST (Western) PUBLICATIONS

QUEST (Western) PUBLICATIONS
The Industrial Estate, Cooks Cross,
South Molton, N. Devon
© S. E. Latham
ISBN 0 905297 01 6

B.B.C. acknowledgements:
        Emily Richard in the title role of the
        B.B.C. serial, Lorna Doone.
        Produced by Barry Letts.
        B.B.C. Copyright photograph by Douglas Playle

        Printed April 1978. Reprinted July 1978.

G. P. Printers, The Industrial Estate, Cooks Cross, S. Molton, Devon.

CONTENTS

The Doones called their Valley "Glen Doone"

RICHARD D. BLACKMORE

When Richard Blackmore was a little boy he used to spend a great deal of his time in the little hamlet of Charles, near South Molton. His grandfather was the vicar, having in earlier years also been the vicar of Oare. It was here he used to tell his grandson the 'nursery tales' about the savage deeds of the outlaw Doones in the depth of Badgworthy Forest, "and the beauty of the hapless maid brought up in the midst of them." From South Molton he would have heard stories of the famous highwayman Tom Faggus, whom many people regarded as a kind of Robin Hood. When Blackmore was twelve he was sent to Blundell's school in Tiverton. There he heard stories of the great big John Ridd, the wrestler from Somerset, and the fight which he had with Robin Snell. These and many more tales of Devon and Somerset he collected together to form the story of Lorna Doone.

Blackmore always called himself a market gardener and he professed to be more proud of his apples and pears than of his novels. Yet Lorna Doone is without doubt still one of the most popular novels in the English Language.

Sir Ensor Doone was the Leader of the Outlaws

CHAPTER 1

ROGUES AND ROBBERS

The story of Lorna Doone begins with John Ridd at Blundell's school in Tiverton, where he tells the story of his fight with Robin Snell. John was getting the worst of it when John Fry, his father's farm worker who had arrived earlier to fetch John home, whispered in his ear, "Never thee knack under, Jan, or never coom naigh Exmoor no more." With these words of warning John got up and soon settled the fight. John Fry had been sent, unknown to John at the time, by his mother, his days at Blundell's school were to end abruptly.

Travelling by packhorse from Tiverton to Dulverton, John and his escort met a lady on a coach, with a little girl of two or three years of age. John continued his journey across Exmoor to Dunkery Beacon, when in the depths of the mist he heard the rattling of chains. Before long he discovered what the noise was. He found the body of a known robber hanging from a gibbet. Still they trudged onward, to be warned within a few miles by John Fry, "Hould thee tongue, lad," he said sharply, "us be naigh the Doone track now." John's little legs were beginning to tremble against Peggy, his horse, as he thought of the dead robber behind him and the live ones in front. They reached a deep goyal (pit) as they call it on Exmoor. John Fry shouted to John to get down from his horse and let her go. Lying on the ground with John Fry bleating like a sheep, they watched the Doones ride past on their horses. John describes them as being heavy men of large stature. They wore leather coats and long boots with iron plates on their breasts and heads. "Plunder was heaped behind their saddles. Some had carcasses of sheep, others had deer and one had a child across his saddle bow." Although John did not know it at the time, the child was the same one he had seen earlier that day in Dulverton.

When John arrived home at Plovers Barrows he was met by his weeping mother who told him that his father had been killed on his way home from Porlock by the dreaded Doones. So John at twelve years of age had the responsibility of the running of the farm.

DUNKERY BEACON

Dunkery Beacon is the highest place on Exmoor, the view from the top is magnificent. The Waterslide used in the B.B.C. serial of Lorna Doone is nearby.

CHAPTER 2

THE DOONES

According to Blackmore, the Doones settled on Exmoor around 1640. They were led by Sir Ensor Doone, who was a rather well-to-do nobleman. He was the joint owner of a large estate in Scotland, but had lost this estate. 'In great despair at last,' he resolved to settle in some outlandish part where none could be found to know him, and decided Exmoor was the ideal place. The Doones settled in a secluded valley not many miles away from John's home at Oare. It was from these headquarters that they undertook their plundering, robberies and murders. Every person on the moor was afraid of them. The Doones carried off many farmers' daughters, "who were sadly displeased at first but after a while settled down and married the robbers." Sir Ensor Doone had one relative whom he called the Counsellor. The Counsellor had one son, the dreaded Carver Doone. It was Carver Doone, the leader of the robbers, who was responsible for the murder of John's father. When we look at Exmoor today it is hard to imagine it as it was in the time of the story. The chief inhabitants of the moor were the wild ponies and the deer. The farmers used it mainly for the keeping of sheep, which were collected from time to time, sorted out and branded at little wooden sheds called the Telling Houses.

John was expecting to meet his father at one of these Telling Houses, and could not understand at the time why his father was not there, until he heard the tragic news from home.

When John turned fourteen years he was quite tall and strong. He decided to try to find some loaches for his mother in the nearby river, so he followed the Badgworthy Waters and as he did so he came across a big water slide. "For lo! I stood at the foot of a long pale slide of water coming smoothly to me, without a break or hindrance for 100 yards or more. And fenced on either side with cliff, sheer, straight and shiny."

John decided he would like to attempt to climb this water slide, not knowing where it would take him. After a long hard struggle he was able to reach the top and quietly he rested by the side of the stream where he eventually went to sleep. When he awoke he found a little girl kneeling at his side, rubbing his forehead tenderly with a dock leaf and handkerchief. She thought John was dead so she was very pleased when he opened his eyes. The little girl told him that her name was Lorna Doone. John had crept into the Doone Valley and was in the midst of the robbers' stronghold. Lorna Doone pleaded with John to go quickly in case they were both killed.

"Why?" wondered John.

"Because," answered Lorna, "you have found your way up here."

John had found a secret way into the Doone Valley.

CHAPTER 3

TOM FAGGUS

One November evening when John was fifteen years old his family were surprised to see their cousin Tom Faggus at their home. Tom Faggus was a highwayman, loved by many people on Exmoor. He was a blacksmith by trade at a little village called North Molton. Tom was engaged to be married to a girl from South Molton called Betsy Paramore, who worked in the George Hotel. Tom was unfairly taken to court by Sir Robert Bampfylde and lost his blacksmith's shop, lands and the girl he loved. He would have also lost his life if he had not decided to become a gentleman of the road. And so Tom said, "The world hath preyed on me like a wolf, God help me to prey on the world."

One day in his course as a highwayman he met up with Sir Bampfylde. Tom took his purse, his ring and timepiece and then with a bow handed them back saying, "it was against any usage to rob a robber." It is said that when he came into an inn all the men liked to meet him, all the women liked to admire him and the children were sent to keep a watch for the law officers.

Tom had a horse called Winnie which was his companion until Tom's final capture and hanging at Taunton. She was a remarkable horse and many times saved Tom's life. Having been a blacksmith

Tom was able to make special shoes for his horse which were round so that if he was chased by the law officers they could not tell for certain which way the horse was going. John Ridd says that when he was with the folk of Exmoor he was very proud to tell them that Tom Faggus was his cousin, but when the parsons or Justices called 'with all these we were very shy of claiming our kinship with that great outlaw.'

TOM FAGGUS'S FORGE NORTH MOLTON
Demolished 1896

THE BAMPFYLDES OF NORTH MOLTON

At North Molton Parish Church there is an alabaster monument to Sir Amyas Bampfylde. The translation reads 'To Sir Amyas Bampfylde Knight, most dear to esteemed father Richard Bampfylde of the ancient Bampfyldes from Poltimore.'

He had twelve sons and five daughters. His eldest son and heir married Elizabeth Drake from Buckland.

CHAPTER 4

MASTER HUCKABACK

John's mother had an Uncle at Dulverton called Reuben Huckaback, who decided to spend New Year tide at Plovers Barrows. Uncle Ben, as John called him, was late in arriving and after a time it was felt that John should try to find where he might be. He says, "The soft white mist came thicker around me as evening fell!" And somewhere in the mist he heard a wheezing noise. "Lord have mercy upon me! O Lord upon my soul have mercy! An' if I cheated Sam Hicks last week, Lord knowest how well he deserved it, and lied in every stocking's mouth—O Lord, where be I a-going?"

John had found Uncle Ben, but alas the Doones had found him first. They had robbed him and tied him upon the back of an Exmoor pony with his feet on the pony's neck and his head to the pony's tail. His arms were hanging down. The wild little pony frightened by its load was racing across the moor, tossing and rolling, trying to remove its burden.

Uncle Ben swearing vengeance on the Doones decided that he would bring them to justice. So with John as his companion, he rode to Lee Manor at Lynton, the home of Baron De Whichehalse to request a warrant against the Doones. Baron De Whichehalse was not as helpful as Uncle Ben had expected him to be so he had to return, without a

"Oh Lord! Where be I a-going?" cried Uncle Huckaback

warrant, and swore that if needs be he would visit the King himself in London. Uncle Ben had yet another trick up his sleeve. He decided to weigh up the possibilities of an attack on the Doone strong-hold.

He decided that he would take John with him to spy out the country of the Doone valley. Although John had seen the valley itself when he climbed the water slide, it was the first time that he was able actually to see clearly the stronghold of the Doones. John described it as "the chine of highland, whereon we stood, curved to the right and left of us, keeping about the same elevation, and crowned with trees and brushwood. At about half a mile in front of us, but looking as if we could throw a stone to strike any man upon it, another crest, just like our own, bowed around to meet it; but failed, by reason of two narrow clefts, of which we could only see the brink. One of these clefts was the Doone-gate, with portcullis of rock above it; and the other was the chasm, by which I had once made an entrance. Betwixt them, where the hill fell back, as in perfect oval, transversed by winding water, lay a bright green valley, rimmed with sheer black rock, and seemingly to have sunken bodily from the bleak rough heights above."

Uncle Ben, regarding himself as the General for the coming attack, then decided which would be the best way to deploy his troops.

CHAPTER 5

JOHN REMEMBERS LORNA

Seeing the Doone stronghold with the Doone gate and his secret waterslide entrance, John again thought of the young girl he had met at the top and her fears for John should he have fallen into the hands of the Doones. With this in mind John decided that he must at all costs make yet another excursion into the dreaded valley. He found the waterslide far less frightening this time and having reached the top he was able to set eyes once again on this young maiden. 'But presently I ventured to look forth, where a bush was; and then beheld the loveliest sight—one glimpse of which was enough to make me kneel in the coldest water.' He found her beauty and gentle manner almost too much for him and realized that he, John Ridd, had fallen in love with Lorna Doone.

He was quite concerned over the matter as he considered himself to be bewitched and so felt it wise to seek the help of Mother Melldrum. Mother Melldrum was a rather strange old lady who was looked on by many Devon and Somerset folk as a witch. Part of the year she lived in a little wooden hut in the Valley of Rocks at Lynton and the remaining part of the year in a cave somewhere near Tarr Steps, a bridge so old that many good Exmoor folk regarded it as the Devil's Bridge.

John at first was terrified of Mother Melldrum and wished that he had stayed at home. 'All this while, the fearful woman was coming near, and more near me; and I was glad to sit down on a rock, because my knees were shaking so.'

Mother Melldrum quietly listened to this story and advised him, "John Ridd, if thou hast any value for thy body or thy soul, thy mother, or thy father's name have nought to do with any Doone." But alas for poor John, it was one thing to seek advice from the poor, old wise woman but another thing for him to follow her counsel.

THE VALLEY OF ROCKS

Blackmore describes the Valley of Rocks as one of the homes of Mother Melldrum. He said, "In winter she lived in a cave within the devil's cheese ring." It is at Lynton and the visitor will also find it interesting to see the wild goats.

CHAPTER 6

JOHN GOES TO LONDON

John made frequent visits to Lorna at the Doone valley, sometimes risking his life as he crept into that stronghold of robbery and violence. After a while Lorna thought it wise to take him to her secret bower and there one day she told him her story, how she met Alan Brandir and of his capture and murder by Carver Doone, and her worst fear of all, which was that one day she was expected to marry Carver Doone. John was particularly concerned to learn that the girl he loved would one day marry the man that killed his father.

Fearing for her life John decided to use some secret signs in case Lorna should ever be in need of his help. But alas these signs were of little avail because shortly after this arrangement Jeremy Stickles the King's messenger, called at John's farm with a command from the King, requesting him to go to London.

Expecting to be away only a week John set off with Jeremy Stickles to Westminster. But alas many weeks were to go by with John waiting in London and nobody caring to see him, until, anxious to be home for the corn harvest, he was ushered into the presence of the Lord Chief Justice Jeffreys. "May it please your worship," said John, "I am here according to order awaiting your good pleasure."

"Thou art made to weight John," replied the Lord Chief Justice. "More than order, how much dost thou tip the scales to?"

"Only twelve score pounds M'Lord, when I be in wrestling trim."

The Lord Chief Justice started questioning John with regard to the Doones. "Now is there in thy neighbourhood a certain nest of robbers, miscreants, and outlaws, whom all fear to handle?"

"Yes," replied John, "I believe some of them to be robbers and all of them to be criminals."

"Then," replied the Lord Chief Justice, "what is your sheriff about that he doth not hang them all?"

"I reckon he is afraid M'Lord, "replied John, "it is not safe to meddle with them."

"What is the name of this pestilent race, and how many are there?"

"They are the Doones of Badgworthy Forest, may it please your worship and we reckon there be about forty of them, beside the women and children."

"Forty Doones, forty thieves and women and children. Thunder of God. How long have they been there then?"

"They may have been there thirty years, M'Lord, before the great war broke out, they came longer back than I can remember."

Looking John straight in the face, screwing his great eyes so that John could not think at all, 'neither look at him nor look away,' Jeffreys asked, "Hast thou ever heard or thought that De Whichehalse is in league with the Doones of Badgworthy?" "Then," asked Jeffreys, changing the subject, "hast thou ever seen a man whose name is Thomas Faggus?"

"Yes, Sir, and many a time. He is my own worthy cousin."

"Tom Faggus is a good man," Jeffreys replied with a smile on his face which showed John that he had met up with Tom.

"I fear he will come to the gallows," he continued, "tell him this for me, Jack, tell him to change his name, turn parson or do something else to make it wrong for me to hang him."

"Is there any sound around your way,' asked Jeffreys, "of disaffection to His Majesty."
"No, M'Lord, no sign whatever," replied John.

There was trouble in store for John, which he never believed possible. The Duke of Monmouth was trying to bring about a rebellion against the King and one of the main reasons why John Ridd had been called to London was to be questioned by the Lord Chief Justice as to the rebellion itself.

"Now John," eventually said Jeffreys after many questions, "I have taken a liking to thee. Keep thou clear of this rebellion my son. It will come to nothing, yet many shall swing high for it. Even I could not save thee John Ridd, if thou wert mixed in this affair. Keep from the Doones, keep away from De Whichehalse, keep away from everything which leads beyond the sight of thy knowledge. I meant to use thee as a tool, but I see thou art too honest and simple. I will send a sharper one down but never let me find thee John, either a tool for the other side or a tube for my words to pass through. Now go thy way Jack, that will do."

CHAPTER 7

HOME AT LAST

John was in London for two months but was able to return in time for harvest. The day after his home-coming, being Sunday, he felt it only right to remain at home with his family in order to meet the many friends and well-wishers from the surrounding farms who came to visit him. When Monday came, however, he decided to leave the men working on the farm and, hoping no-one would dare to follow him, he again ascended the water-slide into the secret bower, once more to meet his beloved Lorna.

He was very distressed to learn that Lorna had had need of him two months earlier. One of the robbers, named Charleworth Doone, was a headstrong gay young man, and the Counsellor decided that Charlie, as everyone called him, was spending too much of his time near Lorna's cottage. So to ensure that he was kept in his proper place, the Counsellor felt that the time had arrived for Lorna to become engaged to Carver Doone, both for Lorna's benefit and for the peace of the family. Lorna would not listen to this suggestion despite Ensor Doone's entreaties and even 'Carver smiled his pleasantest which is truly a frightening thing!' Then both he and his crafty father were for using force with her but Sir Ensor Doone would not hear of it. Lorna was now watched, and spied upon, and nearly all her liberty was taken from her. Poor John did not know what to do. He loved Lorna dearly and the thought of her having to undergo this terrible ordeal was unbearable to him. Then again, he could not be absolutely certain of Lorna's feelings for him.

"Have I caught you, little fish or must all my life be spent in hopeless angling for you?" he had asked her after she had scolded him for trying to place a ring on her finger.

"Neither one nor the other, John. You have not caught me yet altogether, though I like you dearly," she replied.

"Dearest darling of my life," John whispered, "how long must I wait to know?"

PLOVERS BARROWS

Lorna Doone Farm at Malmsmead is generally regarded as the original site of Plovers Barrows. The visitor wishing to walk into the Doone Valley will find a foot path adjoining this farm.

CHAPTER 8

ANNIE & JOHN SHARE SECRETS

The time of the golden harvest had now come and everyone was rejoicing. John could truly say that the harvest had never been so great. And to celebrate this successful year now that the harvest was being gathered in, the first place for festivity was to be Plovers Barrows.

Everyone was invited. Farmer Nicholas Snowe and his three daughters, Parson Bowden, and many others gathered together in the Upper courtyard. First the parson read some verses from the parish Bible telling them all to look up and thank the Lord for all his mercies and the fruits from his land. After a time of rejoicing there was the harvest supper when all could drink their cider, and make merry. Eventually John crept away from the scene of revelry and crossed the court-yard, which was bathed in moonlight, to his father's tomb. There he was startled to see his sister Annie standing motionless, looking so pure and white.

"What are you doing here?" called John.

"I might tell you eventually," replied Annie.

So as John gently coaxed her she led him as far as the old yew tree.

By the yew tree, Annie quietly revealed to him that she had fallen in love herself. At this news John enquired who her young man might be.

Tom Faggus is "only a common highwayman" said John

When Annie accidently mentioned that it was their cousin Tom Faggus, he was furious.

"Only a common highwayman," he answered, "and liable to hang upon any common."

"John," replied his sister, "are the Doones privileged not to be hanged on common land?"

John was thunderstruck, he leapt into the air like a shot rabbit and raced as fast as he could through the gate across the yard and into the kitchen. Desperately he asked Farmer Snowe to give him some tobacco and the loan of a spare pipe. After sitting down for a little while he began to wonder how much of his secret Annie had really discovered. Meanwhile Annie had gone back to her father's grave sobbing quietly, not wishing to trouble any-one. Eventually John returned to her.

"My poor Annie," said John, "have you really promised to be Tom Faggus's wife?"

But Annie was not going to be trapped as easily as John had thought. Instead of answering his questions she asked him if he wished to marry Sally Snowe, 'she gives herself little airs, it is only to entice you, John.' John tried to bring the subject back to Tom Faggus but Annie continued questioning him about Sally.

"Your young maiden is not half as pretty as Sally Snowe," she said.

"She is ten thousand times more pretty than ten thousand Sally Snowes," he replied.

"But look at Sally's eyes," cried Annie.

"Look at Lorna Doone's," replied John, "and you would never again look at Sally's."

"Oh, Lorna Doone, Lorna Doone," exclaimed Annie in triumph. "So Lorna Doone is the lovely maiden who has stolen John Ridd's heart."

For Annie it was a moment of triumph but deep in her own heart her greatest worry was what her mother's reaction would be, when she was told that one of her children was in love with Tom Faggus the highwayman, whilst the other was in love with a member of the family who had murdered her husband. Then to complicate matters even further, Uncle Huckaback had arrived with his grand-daughter Ruth. Both Uncle Huckaback and John's mother had set their hearts on this young lady becoming John's wife.

LEE ABBEY
Lee Abbey situated near the Valley of Rocks was built upon the site of Lee Manor which was once the home of the de Whichehalse family of Lynton.

CHAPTER 9

JOHN AND LORNA

It was one morning in October when John again decided to go into the Doone valley in the hope of seeing Lorna.

"At last then you are come, John. I thought you had forgotten me," said Lorna as she approached him.

"You know what I have come to ask," replied John after a slight pause.

"If you have come on purpose to ask anything, why did you delay so?"

Lorna turned away bravely but John could see that her lips were trembling. "I waited so long because I fear my whole life hangs on the balance of a single word," John replied.

As he continued to speak Lorna trembled more and more, but she made no answer and neither would she look at John.

"I have loved you long and long," he continued, "when you were a small child, as a boy I worshipped you, when I saw you as a comely girl I adored you and now that you are full grown all the rest I do and more. I love you more than tongue can tell."

"You have been faithful John," she replied, "I suppose I must reward you."

"That will not do for me," John said, "I will have no reluctant liking. I must have all your love or none.

I must have your heart of hearts as you have mine, Lorna."

"Darling," she replied, "you have won it all. I shall never be my own again. I am yours, my only one, for ever and for ever."

John's heart was full of emotion. What he said and did then he could neither remember nor care. All he knew was that Lorna Doone loved him and that he slipped a little ring upon her wedding finger. This time Lorna kept it. She then gave John a ring as a token of her love for him.

Some time later he returned home, having promised Lorna that he would tell his mother everything. John had little doubt in his mind that his mother would be very upset.

Unfortunately his good intentions came to nothing, for sitting down at breakfast, with his mother, was Tom Faggus. As soon as the meal was over John had to go ploughing. When he returned Lizzie came running to meet him crying, "Oh John, there has been such a business. Mother is in such a state of mind and Annie crying her eyes out. What do you think? You would never guess, though I have suspected it ever so long."

John could indeed guess the cause of the trouble.

"Oh, John, speak one good word for me," cried Annie, as his mother shouted for him.

"And you won't tell her about Lorna, not to-day, dear," she continued.

"Yes, to-day," he replied, "and at once. I want to have it over."

Bravely John explained to his mother everything

concerning Lorna and himself. Quietly he stood by whilst his mother said many things he would not dare to repeat concerning the Doones, but by the evening she was sitting on the garden bench with her right arm around Annie's waist, not knowing which of her children to make the most of. Both John and Annie knew that they had won over their mother, so they let her lay down the law in her own, maternal way.

TARR STEPS
The age of the clapper bridge at Tarr Steps is a matter of debate. Many experts claim that the original must be as old as Stonehenge. It is certainly an ancient monument. It is situated near Dulverton.

CHAPTER 10

A DESPERATE VENTURE

John did not see Lorna again for quite a while, and being anxious to discover what might have happened to her he resolved that he would creep in through the Doone gate to where Lorna lived. It was a very perilous journey and as John slipped through the gate there were many moments when he thought his end had come.   He found it necessary to hide from the sentries for many hours.   Eventually he managed to reach the house in which Lorna lived. As she opened the rough lattice he whispered gently

"O Lorna, don't you know me?"

"John," she cried, "you must be mad, John."

"As mad as a march hare without any news from his darling," he replied.

Later John whispered "Tell me what means all this. Why are you penned up here? Are you in any danger?"

Lorna replied, "My poor grandfather is very ill and the Counsellor and his son are now masters of the valley. I dare not go out." Lorna then introduced John to little Gwenny Carfax who promised John that she would henceforth act as their messenger. "But how shall I know your danger now?" John asked.

Lorna paused for a moment, "John I have been thinking about this, can you see the tree with the seven rooks' nests bright against the cliffs? Can you count them from above? From a place where you will be safe dear?" Lorna asked.

"No doubt I can, or if I can't it will not take me long to find a spot where I can do so," he replied.

"Gwenny can climb like a cat," continued Lorna, "she has been up there in the summer, watching the birds day after day. If you see six rooks' nests I will be in trouble and will need your help. If you see five nests I will have been carried off by Carver Doone."

John was terrified at this last thought.

"Fear not, John," Lorna whispered, "I have means to stop him, or at least save myself. If you can come within one day of that man getting hold of me you will find me quite unharmed, but after that you will find me dead or alive, according to the circumstances, but in no case such that you need blush to look at me."

One evening, a little while after John's brave venture into the Doones' stronghold, he was walking his usual circuit of the hills, with his dog, Watch, who suddenly gave a long, low growl. John could see a small figure, in the moonlight at Plovers Barrows. He was delighted to discover that it was the little maid, Gwenny Carfax.

"Young man," she said as she came up to John, "please come with me, old man be dying and he can't die, or at least won't, without first considering thee."

"Considering me?" John replied, "What can Sir Ensor Doone want with me? Has Lorna told him?"

"All things concerning thee and thy doings when she knowed old man was coming to his end," Gwenny told him.

Although the thought of meeting Sir Ensor Doone frightened John, he knew that he must either go to see the old man or give up Lorna once and for all. So, with great misgiving in his heart, he made his way with Gwenny across the moor, through a secret passage-way and into Sir Ensor Doone's house. As they came to the door his heart was thumping madly, the reason for which he was not quite certain—the dread of meeting Sir Ensor Doone or the joy of seeing Lorna once more. In a moment this fear was quite gone as Lorna trembled in his arms.

"Ah!" said the old man, as Lorna left them together "are you that great John Ridd?

"John Ridd is my name, your honour, and I hope your worship is better," said John, not knowing what else to answer.

"Child have you sense enough to know what you have been doing? Are you ignorant of the fact that Lorna Doone was born of one of the oldest families in Europe and you know of your low descent from the Ridds of Oare," continued Sir Ensor.

"Sir," replied John, "the Ridds of Oare have been honest men twice as long as the Doones have been rogues."

"I would not answer for that," replied Sir Ensor. "If it be so, thy family is the very oldest in Europe." After a further exchange of words the old man said,

"I want you to pledge your word in Lorna's

presence, never to see or seek her again, nor even to think of her any-more. Now call her for I am weary." John went back into the other room where Lorna was crying softly by the window. John laid his arm around her to comfort her, and then once again they entered together the presence of Sir Ensor Doone, with Lorna's right hand swallowed in the palm of John's. Sir Ensor looked astonished. For forty years he had been feared and obeyed by all around him.

"You two fools," he said, "you two fools."

"May it please your worship," John replied, "may be we are not such fools as we look."

"Fools you are," Sir Ensor replied, "be fools for ever, it is the best thing I can wish you. Boy and girl, be boy and girl, until you have grown children."

John remained in Sir Ensor's room for a little longer. Eventually the old man let his hand drop downwards and crooked his little finger.

"He wants something out of the bed, dear," Lorna whispered to John, "see what it is, it's upon your side." John followed the curve of the old man's shrunken hand and felt among the pillows. There he found a beautiful necklace.

"Why it's my glass necklace," Lorna cried with great surprise. "My necklace which he always promised me and from which you got the ring, John." She gave it to him for safe-keeping. Shortly after, Sir Ensor Doone died and was buried in Doone valley. John remained for the funeral but was then very relieved to return to the safety of Plovers Barrows.

CHAPTER 11

THE GREAT WINTER

The winter of that year was one of the hardest John had ever known and a great deal of his time was taken up going with John Fry and some other helpers to find their lost sheep and then digging them out of the snow. Despite this hard rescue work, John still lost half of his flock. Even the horses, mustering together in the stables, had long icicles hanging from their muzzles nearly every morning. However, this could not stop John from worrying, because of the impossibility, due to the weather, of either hearing or having any token from his beloved. It snowed during the day then each night it would clear and freeze, isolating every valley on the moor.

Lizzie, as John called his other sister, used to enjoy reading a lot of books. One day she told John how the Eskimos made special shoes for walking over the snow. This gave John an idea. He managed to build himself a pair of light snow shoes made of ash and ribbed with withy, with half tanned skins stretched across on the inner sole to support his feet. First of all he was unable to walk in these; but after a great deal of practice falling down and picking himself up several times, he walked across the farm yard and back. The following day, with his mother's blessing, he decided that he would risk the elements and try to get into the Doone valley to see if Lorna was well, the rooks' nests were gone.

The snow had started to fall again, it seemed thick enough to blind a man, John thought this would be good cover for him until he reached Lorna's house. Not knowing if Lorna was inside, he decided to venture to the door and knock, not certain whether his answer would be the barrel of a gun or Lorna's sweet voice. Fortunately he was safe, for he heard the pattering of feet and a shrill voice through the latch hole saying, "Who's there?"

"Only me, John Ridd," he replied,

"Put your finger through the latch hole young man, with the ring that Lorna gave you on it, but mind you if it be the wrong one thou shalt never draw it back again."

Laughing at Gwenny's mighty threat John showed his finger by the opening; upon seeing the ring she let him in.

"Us be shut in here," exclaimed Gwenny, "and starving. I wish thou wert good to eat young man, I would manage most of thee."

John noticed the way she was looking at him, and decided to give her a loaf of bread, which Gwenny leapt upon as a starving dog leaps upon its supper. Whilst John was removing his snow shoes he watched her run around the corner to her young mistress with it. Lorna had fainted from hunger, and John carefully nursed her back to her senses. "I never expected to see you again. I made up my mind to die, John, without you knowing it," she said.

Then, as she placed her weak little hand in John's, he could not stem the flow of his tears as he saw the terrible plight that she was in. Gently he fed her, as he asked the meaning of all this.

"The meaning is sad enough," said Lorna, "I see no way out of it. We are to be starved until I let them do what they want with me."

Then, John with thudding heart, as he considered the terrible danger he was about to enter into, asked Lorna, "If I were to take you to safety without much fright or hardship, Lorna, would you come with me?"

"To be sure I will," she replied. "The alternatives are small, either to starve, or go with you, John."

"Gwenny, have you the courage for it, will you come with your young mistress?"

"Will I stay behind?" said a voice which truly confirmed her loyalty. By this time the snow had subsided somewhat, and Lorna called to John,

"Come to the frozen window, John. You will see them light the stack fire, you stay in that corner dear and I will stand on this side: and try to breathe yourself a peep hole through the spars and banners. Oh, you don't know how to do it. I must do it for you. Breathe three times like that, and then you must rub it with your fingers before it has time to freeze again. They are firing Dunkery Beacon to celebrate their new captain."

John felt that this would be the ideal time to take Lorna back to Plovers Barrows.

"Sweetest, I will return in two hours time for you. Have Gwenny ready to answer. You are safe whilst they are dining, drinking healths, and all that stuff and before they have done with that I shall be with you. Pack everything you need to take, when I return I shall knock loudly once, wait, and then knock softly twice.''

As quickly as possible John hurried back to the farm by way of the waterslide where he had made so many excursions into the valley. To his great delight there was hardly any snow there at all. His waterslide was now a path of ice. This made an easy track over which he felt he could guide his old sledge, with Lorna riding upon it.

Arriving at the farm he went to the shed to collect his light pony sledge. He girded his own body with a dozen strands of rope, joining the ends to the sledge, while his mother and sisters were busy packing blankets and a sealskin cloak. Then he hurried to the frozen water slide. There he left the sledge, crossed the valley and knocked on the door as planned. No-one came, so he knocked even louder, but again he received no answer. He then threw all his weight against the door so gaining entrance. He found Lorna crouching behind a chair with her hands up to her face. In the middle of the room lay Gwenny almost senseless, yet still with one hand clutching the ankle of a struggling man. Another man was standing above Lorna trying to pull the chair away. In a moment John grabbed hold of him around the waist and threw him out of the window with a mighty crash of breaking glass. Then he took the other man by the throat stifling his pleas for mercy, and took him outside, squeezing his throat a little more as he did so. He would have killed him if he had not noticed by the moonlight that it was Marwood De Whichehalse. John then looked for the other fellow that he had thrown through the window and eventually found Charlie Doone lying stunned and bleeding. He then knew that there was no time to linger. Quickly he caught up Lorna and, calling Gwenny to follow him, ran the whole distance across the valley to the sledge. They made their way through the cleft, down the water-slide and back to the farm. By the time they got there Lorna was unconscious.

As the family ran to meet them John shouted to his mother, "You shall see her first. Is she not your daughter?"

His mother's hands were trembling as she open-ed the seal-skin cloak. She bent down and kissed Lorna's forehead saying; "God bless her, John." After this they carried Lorna, who was still uncon-scious, into the house and placed her upon the couch near the fire.

"All go away except Mother." John shouted.

"The frost is in her brain, I have heard of this before, John", she whispered.

"Mother," he replied, "I will have it out, leave her to me altogether. You sit there and watch." Whereupon he sat gently by her and held her in his arms. After a while her eyes began to brighten and her small entreating hands found their way into the protection of his great palms and, trembling, rested there. 'As Mother looked upon us, all she could say was "God bless you, my sweet child." '

CHAPTER 12

THE DOONES ATTACK

Life seemed to take on a new meaning for John now that Lorna was with him daily. She on her part would not sit idly by and let John's mother and sisters wait on her, but always busied herself in the kitchen.

The Doones, however, were not prepared to accept this conquest of the lovely lady. One day John arrived home at Plovers Barrows to find the whole house in an uproar. The previous evening Lorna had gone out into the garden, when she saw two glittering eyes staring at her, she recognised the face of Carver Doone. Although Lorna had been used to terror, she completely lost all presence of mind. She could neither shriek nor run but could only stand frozen to the spot in horror as she watched Carver grinning hideously whilst pointing his gun at her heart. She would have liked to have put up her hand to defend herself but it seemed as if every part of her was frozen

Showing no pity he slowly lowered the gun between the arches of Lorna's feet and pulled the trigger, then as she fell back on the grass, he exclaimed, "I have spared you this time only because it suits my plan, but unless you come back to-morrow and teach me to destroy the fool who has destroyed himself for you, your death is here where it has long been waiting!"

He rode away not even caring to look back.

Expecting the Doones to attack that night John sent all the women to bed early, except for Gwenny Carfax and John Fry's wife, Betty, in the hope that these two would be useful. Jeremy Stickles had helped to muster together a few men and they prepared themselves for the fray. John did not remain in the house, having remembered that it was a custom of the Doones to light the straw ricks before they started their rampaging and plundering. He betook himself to the rick yard, but suddenly being overcome by sleep he sat down and was lost to the world until he felt a light hand upon his arm.

"Who's that?" he said, "Stand up and let me have a fair chance at you."

"Are you going to knock me down, dear John?"

"My darling," John replied, "is it you breaking orders? Go back into the house at once."

"But how can I sleep?" replied Lorna, "when at any moment you might be killed underneath my window. The man at the back of the house is asleep, he has been snoring for two hours, Gwenny heard him when she came with me. I think the women ought to keep watch as they have had no travelling."

It was finally agreed that little Gwenny Carfax should watch from a nearby tree, from where she could see the Barrow valley. She would be able to see the Doones crossing the stream in the moonlight. It was not long before she came running back shouting, "Ten of them crossed the water, down yonner."

Quickly John sent her back to the house asking her to fetch Jeremy Stickles and all the men while he stayed behind to guard the ricks.

Eventually the Doones rode into the yard as coolly as if they had been personally invited. Carver Doone shouted, "Two of you lazy fellows go and make a light to cut their throats by. If any man touches Lorna I will stab him where he stands. Kill every man and every child and burn the cursed place down."

Presently two men made their way towards the ricks not noticing John behind one of them. As the first set his torch to the rick within a yard of John, he struck him down to the ground. The other man stood in amazement not knowing how his mate had fallen, but as John snatched the fire brand from his hand he leapt at him, only to find that John had gripped him in a wrestling hold and had snapped his collar bone. Within a moment there was a blaze of gun fire as the villains came swaggering down in the moonlight, ready for murder. Two of them came on, whilst the others hung back. John was able to grasp Carver Doone by the beard, and hissed, "Do you call yourself a man?"

Within a moment he had laid him flat on his back. Seeing their leader down, all of the men fled, some on horseback and others on foot leaving their horses behind. Eventually Carver Doone quietly escaped and got back to the stronghold. Jeremy Stickles thought it unwise to continue the pursuit any further.

Carver Doone shouted, "Two of you make a light to cut their throats by."

Already two of the Doones had been killed and two had been taken prisoner.

Despite all this John received many visits from the Doones. One day he had a visit from the Counsellor himself. Despite his clever tricks and entreaties, John would not dare to think of letting Lorna return to that cruel man and his band of robbers.

A HALF SAVAGE RACE

Several half savage races of men have tried to settle on Exmoor and the immediate area. One such race was called the "Gubbins". They were said to have been so stupid that instead of using a chair they would sit on the ground and dig a hole to put their feet in!

CHAPTER 13

DEVONS AGAINST SOMERSETS

All the farmers in the surrounding district were beginning to lose patience, and, with Jeremy Stickles' help and leadership it was decided to make an all-out attack on the Doone stronghold. The plan of attack was the same as the one Uncle Ben Huckaback had suggested a while before. Jeremy Stickles managed to muster together a group of both Devon and Somerset Yeoman. The Somerset men he called his 'Yellow boys' and the men from Devon his 'Red boys'. Together these numbered one hundred and twenty men, besides which they had fifteen troopers from the regular army.

On the appointed day they all made their way with guns and cannons to the Doone Valley. The Devon brigade marched to the western side of the valley, and the Somerset contingent stayed upon the eastern highland, where they were not to show themselves until their cousins from Devon were in position at the parapet of the glen. The fifteen troopers, with ten men all hand picked from the 'reds and yellows' were to assault the main gate itself. These were led by Jeremy Stickles and John, who together controlled the tactics for the grand campaign which was to drive the Doones into the centre of the valley. Should they seek to escape via the gate these hand picked soldiers were ready for them with their guns.

At last they heard a loud 'bang'. This was the signal that the Devon and Somerset men were in position and pouring their cannon upon the valley. The sound of the men's cheers echoed through the air but in the midst of the cheering disaster struck. The trunk of a tree had been thrown by the Doones among John and his men. Then five or six of the Doones with their guns blasting away rushed in. Several of John's men were struck by the explosion of the cannon and as they fled for shelter they were met by a young boy shouting, ''You had better be off, all of you, Somerset and Devon are fighting and the Doones have thrashed them both.''

It would seem that the men of Devon had a long way to go around the hills to their agreed position, and fearing that the Somerset men would receive all the glory, they did not wait to take good aim with their cannon, but upon seeing the others about to shoot, they started to fire first. The shot was a mixture of anything considered hard, such as jug bottoms and door knobs, etc., and all of this landed amongst the unfortunate Somerset men killing one and injuring two. The Somerset men did not wait for their friends' 'beg your pardon' but trained their gun full-mouth upon them with a vicious shot and cheered to see four or five of the Devons fall.

The Doones laughed to see the thunder passing overhead as their would-be attackers attacked themselves. Then they made their way from the valley and fell on the rear of the Somerset men, killing four of them as they stood beside their cannon. As the survivors ran away the Doones took the hot culverin and rolled it into their valley. Out of three great guns only one remained which was the one belonging to the Devons, who dragged it back themselves so that they might boast of it. The two Devon officers then took command and ordered all of the men to return to their own homes.

LANDACRE BRIDGE

CHAPTER 14

JEREMY SPIES THE COUNTRY

Lord Chief Justice Jeffreys, true to his word, decided to spy out the land with regard to the Doones and the coming rebellion by the Duke of Monmouth.

One who was by now John's true friend, Jeremy Stickles, was sent back to Exmoor by Lord Jeffreys. As he spied out the land there were many times when his life was in danger, but somehow he always managed to escape both robbers and the leaders of the rebellion.

One of these narrow escapes was when Carver Doone was waiting with a group of his companions to ambush him. John Ridd was cutting wood nearby when he overheard their plans. He managed to slip away and warn Jeremy of the danger.

A similar incident took place when Jeremy had been in the town of South Molton. Finding the roads impassable with floods he had made his way to Landacre bridge, accompanied by a single trooper. As they approached the water of the River Barle, which was pouring down in a mighty torrent, Jeremy took to the river and swam his horse across. As he turned to watch the trooper's passage he heard the report of a gun behind him and felt a pain such as to lift him from his saddle. Looking behind he saw three men, two of whom were ready to reload and the third was aiming to shoot again. Jeremy, lying flat on the neck of his horse, turned back and charged straight at this man, who fired his gun again. Jeremy then aimed his pistol at the largest man and made his escape through Withycombe finally returning to Plovers Barrows only to realize that his companion had been either shot or drowned.

During this time Tom Faggus was at Plovers Barrows and the subject of Lorna's little 'Trinket', as she called the necklace, was raised. This had been in John's care since his visit to Sir Ensor Doone. After a while Tom asked if he could see the 'Trinket', so Annie quickly fetched Lorna and then John's mother led her into the light for Tom to examine it. Tom Faggus took it eagerly and carried it to the window. After a while he jokingly asked,

"What will you take for it, Mistress Lorna?"

"I am not accustomed to selling things, Sir," she replied.

"What is it worth in you opinion? Do you think it is worth five pounds?" enquired Tom.

"On no, I've never had so much money in all my life. It is very pretty but cannot be worth five pounds, I am sure."

"What a chance for a bargain," Tom exclaimed, "if it were not for Annie I could make my fortune. There are twenty-five rose diamonds in it and twenty-five large brilliants which cannot be matched in London. How say you, Mistress Lorna, to £100,000?"

At this Lorna's eyes flashed brighter than any diamond and taking it gently from Tom she went to John's mother and said, "Dear mother, now you shall have it, won't you dear? And I shall be happy, for a thousandth part of your kindness to me no jewel in the world can match".

One day a little later Jeremy was told the story of the necklace, and how Lorna came to have it.

Just before the attack by the Doones he came upon a dark, foreign-looking woman at Watchet. She was Italian by birth and told Jeremy how she had come to be in the region. Once she had been nursemaid to a Scottish noble-family and with them she had travelled over the main parts of Europe. They had landed on the Devonshire coast and stayed some days at Exeter. Leaving Exeter they travelled into Somerset on their way to Watchet, where the lady owned a quiet mansion. However, on the following morning, with the mud being soft and deep, the heavy coach broke down and they had to stop for repairs at Dulverton, where they lost three hours or more. The coach journeyed on and on through the fog and mud, but then, thanking God, they came to the outskirts of the town of Watchet. They noticed a troop of horsemen waiting behind a nearby rock ready to dash upon them. Bravely the lady stood up in the coach as the driver rode into the sea until the front horses were swimming.

Before the waves came into the coach a score of fierce men were around it, seeing one of them the lady cried out, "I know that man, he is our ancient enemy!" Then a great wave came in the coach and it was thrown on its side. What followed the Italian woman did not know as she was stunned by a blow on the head, but when she recovered she found that the little girl was missing. Her lady was sitting upright on a rock with her dead son's head on her bosom, sometimes gazing upon him and sometimes looking around searching for the little girl. The lady was taken to Watchet where she died and lies buried in Watchet's little churchyard with her son and heir at her right hand and a little babe of sex unknown sleeping on her bosom. The little girl was never found.

As John listened to the story of the heavy coach, and the breakdown at Dulverton, his heart broke within him. He remembered his journey as a boy from Blundell's school with John Fry, the coach he had met at Dulverton and his night upon the moor when he saw the Doones ride by with their plunder and the little maiden who was carried upon the back of one of the horses. When Jeremy spoke of the necklace thrown over the head of the little maiden John realized that this little girl was his very own Lorna Doone.

Eventually Lorna was introduced to her nurse-maid and it was confirmed that she was indeed a lady of great substance. Her Uncle was appointed her guardian and master until she was twenty-one years old.

It was a very sad day for John when it was decided that Lorna must leave Plovers Barrows and live in London with her guardian. As she left, Lorna promised John that she would never forget him and she would write every day, but alas the months went by for John without a word or note from his beloved.

CHAPTER 15

LORNA IS STILL LORNA

John did not see or hear from Lorna for over a year. He felt she must have forgotten him for surely, he reckoned, she would at least have written once.

One day when he was in London he met her, whereupon he was invited to her home at Earl Brandir's house.

"Darling Lorna, Lady Lorna," he cried when they were alone.

"Yes it is, John, nothing else. Why have you behaved so?"

" I am behaving", John replied, "to the best of my ability. There is no other man in the world who could hold you so without kissing you."

"Then why don't you do it, John?" replied Lorna looking at him with a flash of her old fun.

"Master John Ridd," she eventually asked, "why have you never for more than a year taken the smallest notice of your old friend Lorna Doone?"

"Simply for this cause, my old friend and true love took not the smallest heed of me, nor knew I where to find her."

"What," cried Lorna, "Oh, you poor John." With these words she pulled a cord and Gwenny Carfax came in with a grave sullen face.

"Gwenny," began Lorna, "go and fetch the letters I gave you at various times to despatch to

Mr. Ridd". And although Gwenny tried to make excuses, it soon became evident that she had been placing the letters to one side, instead of posting them on Lorna's behalf to John.

Angrily Lorna shouted at Gwenny: "Much gratitude you have shown to Master Ridd for his kindness after he had risked his own life to save your father when you had lost him for months and months."

"What made you treat me so, Gwenny?" John asked.

"Because you're below her so," replied Gwenny, "her shan't have a poor farming chap. Even if he were a Cornish man."

"Gwenny, you may go!" exclaimed Lorna, trembling with anger.

Lorna had to remain in her guardian's care well after Sedgemoor was over, but eventually the Lady Lorna Dugal, which was her rightful name, was able to set aside much of her wealth, land and title to return to John at Plovers Barrows as his own Lorna Doone.

CHAPTER 16

SEDGEMOOR

One day Tom Faggus rode into Plovers Barrows with some good news to tell, and he told it with such force of expression that it made everyone laugh. Apparently he was now a Squire and had purchased a good piece of land in the parish of Molland from Sir Roger Bassett. Tom said that when the lawyers realized who he was and how he had made his money, they treated him uncommonly well and showed great sympathy for his pursuits.

His greatest pride of all was to be able to invite Annie to sit at the table with a man who held the King's pardon. They were eventually married and their first years together were full of bliss, particularly for Annie when she had her first child.

(The expected rebellion against the King took place and finally ended in the Battle of Sedgemoor near Bridgwater).

One day at the beginning of July, John had come home from a morning's mowing to fetch fresh supplies of cider, when he noticed, in the courtyard, a little cart of the type which few men in the country used. Annie had returned to the farm to beg John's help as "Tom had gone off with the rebels and you must go after him," she pleaded.

Moved as he was by Annie's tears, John was in no particular hurry to be found near the Duke of Monmouth's men.

After a great deal of persuasion John made his way through the town of Dulverton, arriving at Bridgwater on the fifth or sixth of July. He found half of the town full of the good Duke's men.

After having sought for Tom in vain, he went to an hotel and fell fast asleep. He was aroused by the landlady pulling and pinching him.

"Can't you leave me alone?" he grumbled.

"Wish to God, young man, that I could," she answered, "Get up! Go and fight! We can hear the battle already."

"I am for King James if any," replied John.

"Then thou may'st for ever stop in bed," muttered the old woman sulkily.

But fearing for Tom's life and remembering his promise to Annie, John got up in the early hours and made his way to the battle-field. Here he searched through the terrible carnage without success. As he dismounted to aid some of the wounded he felt warm lips laid against his cheek. It was Tom's horse leaning over him and if ever a horse tried to speak it was Winnie at that moment. Eventually she ran away to another part of the field with John following her until she entered the doorway of a low black shed. There he found her sniffing gently at the body of Tom Faggus who groaned feebly as John raised him up. There was a savage wound in Tom's right side. After bandaging this as best he could John set Tom upon Winnie and, after placing his feet in the stirrups, told him to lean forward. Tom then shouted, "God bless you, John. I am safe, for who can come near my Winnie?

One mile of her gallop is ten years of life." He whistled and the mare went eagerly forward as swift as a swallow.

However, John was not so fortunate. Just after these events he fell into the hands of Colonel Kirk and his Lambs, who would have hanged him there and then. He was taken to the fatal tree where two men were already dangling and John would have joined them had it not been for the timely intervention of Captain Stickles, (as Jeremy was called in time of war). As John shook his hand Jeremy said: "Turn for good turn! You saved my life from the Doones, and, by the mercy of God, I have saved you from far worse company."

As for poor Tom, he managed to reach safety but because of his involvement with Sedgemoor his pardon was recalled. Some say that he was finally caught at an inn and hanged at Taunton. Others maintain that he managed to keep the law at a distance until he was at last granted another pardon. One such tale supporting this is that he was one day trapped upon Barnstaple Bridge with soldiers at either end of it. As they hesitated to approach him he jumped to the left hand parapet on his strawberry mare, Winnie, and whispered in her dove coloured ear. Without a moment's hesitation she leapt into the foaming tide and swam to safety.

There are many more stories that could be told concerning Tom Faggus but space will not permit in this little book.*

*Quest (Western) Publications are producing a novel based on the life of Tom Faggus.

John and Lorna received many visits from the Doones

CHAPTER 17

THE DOONES MUST GO

Local Farmers and yeomen at last resolved that a further assault must be made upon the Doone Valley. One night all the forces joined together, taking whatever weapons of war they could lay their hands upon. They made their way quietly into the valley and set fire to the logwood house where Carver Doone lived. John regarded this as his special privilege and he had insisted on the exclusive right that no other flint should be used against it but his own. Taking good care not to harm any innocent women and children, they burnt down two or three more houses. Carver had ten or twelve wives and many felt that this may have been the reason that he took the loss of Lorna so easily! However, John noticed one child, a fair and handsome little fellow, who was beloved by Carver above anyone or anything, and as the boy climbed onto his back for safety John felt that he could not do, or say, anything to hurt him.

Before long they had managed to set fire to most of the village and in the confusion the Doones believed there must be at least one hundred soldiers. "All Doone Town is on fire!" they exclaimed as they sought a way of escape. All the valley was flooded with light, and as the Doones made their way, recklessly of their end, the farmers would not wait for any word of command before they shot at the men they abhorred. Only Carver and a few other Doones escaped the carnage of that night.

SEDGEMOOR—THE LAST BATTLE ON ENGLISH SOIL

King Charles II died in 1685. James II, his brother who succeeded him was very unpopular. He was challenged by his nephew, the Duke of Monmouth, the illegitimate son of Charles II, for the sovereignty of England. Monmouth landed in England at Lyme Regis and made his way through Taunton to Bridgwater where he was proclaimed King. But some of the enthusiasm of his followers waned and they deserted in their hundreds. Meanwhile the King's men were encamped on Sedgemoor near the little villages of Weston Zoyland and Chedzoy.

Monmouth and his men left Bridgwater at approximately 10.30 a.m., on Sunday 5th July, 1685 and marched along the Bath road to Bradney and then turned to the right to reach the Moor. Their surprise attack failed and a pistol was fired to give the alarm. The Battle commenced at 1.30 on the morning of the 6th July, 1685 and lasted only one and a half hours. The King's men led by Lord Faversham continued until dawn to shoot the rebels for sport. Then the town of Bridgwater was turned over to the tender mercy of Colonel Kirk and his Lambs. It was a savage vengeance and the road to Bridgwater was lined with gallows. Over five hundred prisoners were brought to Weston Zoyland Church, later to face trial at Taunton. This later became known as the 'bloody assize' for three hundred executions took place and eight hundred prisoners were transported on the orders of Judge Jeffreys.

The battlefield is worth seeing as it is one of the few places that one can imagine the battle taking place.

A monument at the battle site reads: 'To the Glory of God and in the memory of all those who doing the right thing as they gave it, fell in the Battle of Sedgemoor 6th July, 1685 and lie here buried in this field or who for their share suffered death or transportation. Pro Patria.'

The Duke of Monmouth was beheaded on July 15th, 1685. Ironically King James' reign lasted only three more years; William of Orange landed in England to bring about the 'glorious revolution' on November 5th, 1688.

CHAPTER 18

LORNA IS SHOT

Lorna was now at home with John permanently and they arranged the day for their wedding at Oare Church. John's mother was thrilled as she helped with these arrangements.

Lizzie and Annie, together with all the people from the surrounding district, came to the church that day and as Lorna walked down the aisle in all her beauty John was almost too afraid to look at her. She was dressed in white, clouded with lavender, yet with a simplicity which did not detract from her loveliness. The service took its usual form and as John placed the ring upon her finger the parson blessed them on their marriage. Lorna then turned to John with a playful glance of fun which deepened with this solemn act. They were about to kiss each other for the first time as husband and wife, she looking lovingly into his eyes when the sound of a shot rang through the church and Lorna's eyes went dim with death. She fell across his knees and he lifted her up to pet and coax her, but it was no use. The only sign of life remaining was the drip of bright red blood upon the altar. As everyone raced forward John laid his wife in his mother's arms and begged no-one to make a noise as he went for his revenge. He jumped on his horse and although he was not armed, he thought over

A shot rang through the Church

and over again, "Thy life or mine as the will of God may be, we two shall not live on this earth one more hour together."

At last he came to Black Barrow Down, where he saw a little distance ahead of him a man with a child on a black horse—Carver Doone. He knew full well the strength of the man and that he still held a gun and sword, yet John was still convinced that he could kill him. Rushing through the crag all John could see was that brutal deed, and feel piteous anguish and cold despair.

Carver turned up the valley leading to Cloven Rocks, but as he entered it, he saw that John was only one hundred yards behind him, so he thrust his spurs into his horse, and a cry of triumph rose with a vile oath from the black depths of his heart. Finding that he had no room in the rocky channel to turn and fire, Carver plunged into the black ravine leading to the Wizard's Slough. Suddenly he turned the corner into the black bog and, with a start of fear, reined back his horse, then rode carefully on hoping to find a way around. Finding none, he turned and fired at John and charged at him with his sword. The bullet hit John, but he took no notice of it, his only fear being Carver's escape. Then with the limb of an oak John struck Carver's horse full on the forehead, before the slash of his sword came near. Both men then rolled over on the ground.

Carver was somewhat stunned, whilst John leapt to his feet and bared his arms as one would in the ring for wrestling. He then shouted to Carver's son, "Run up yonder around the corner to find bluebells for the pretty lady."

As the child ran away Carver shouted to John: "I will not harm you, lad, I have punished you enough", but John's only answer was to slap him across the face, whereupon Carver caught John around the waist with such a grip that John heard his ribs snap. John in rage grasped Carver's arm and tore its muscle out. Then, grabbing Carver by the throat as he tried to push his fist into John's face, he shouted, "I will not harm thee anymore, Carver Doone, thou art beaten, own it, and thank God for it. Only go thy way and repent thyself."

But it was too late. Carver had fallen into the bog and as its sucking started to pull him under, John could only stand back and gaze, for his strength was no more than an infant's. Throughout this horror he could scarcely look away as Carver vanished joint by joint, screaming for help as that black bog sucked him under.

When the little boy returned from picking flowers the only sign left of his father was a dark brown bubble on a patch of blackness. Out of love and pity John then took him back to Plovers Barrows.

When he came to the stable door John, falling from his horse, was helped into the farmhouse by John Fry. "I have killed him," was all that he could say, "as he killed Lorna. Let me look at her, Mother, she belongs to me none the less though she is dead."

All the women fell away whispering and sobbing, looking with side glances at John's face which was as hard as flint.

"You can't see her now, John." Ruth replied,

"She is not your dead one, she may even be your live wife, home and happiness, but you must not let her see you like that."

For days they both lay on the verge of death, Lorna kept alive through the constant care of Ruth, whilst John was under the care of his doctor. One day he was sitting in his bedroom when he heard a knock at the door.

"Can you receive visitors, cousin Ridd?"

It was Ruth. "Why!" she exclaimed, "They never told me of this, I knew that you were weak, dear John but not dying." When she was told that the doctor visited twice a week to bleed him, she decided that she would look after him herself.

Some time later Ruth knocked on the door as before, but this time ran away leaving Lorna standing before him. As she threw her arms around him John felt his trust in God revive with the joy of living and of loving dearer things than life. As for Lorna, she never tired of being with John and talking together of the fears, troubles, dangers and bitter partings they used to undergo.

So the story ends. Lorna was indeed John's life-long love. Year by year he watched her beauty grow with the growth of their happiness and love.

John saw Carver Doone riding ahead of him

CHAPTER 19

THE FILMING OF LORNA DOONE

Mr. Barry Letts, the producer of the 1976 B.B.C. dramatisation of Lorna Doone, avoided the usual Hollywood extravaganza of a big, non-existent, castle in a valley about the size of the Grand Canyon in America. As near as possible, he kept to the actual story, and where he could, to the exact location. To find a place which would at least match the story as narrated by Blackmore, one or two sites needed to be changed. His description of the Doone Gate does not fit any place on Exmoor exactly, so the location chosen for this was near the Cheddar Gorge.

The waterslide at the Doone Valley bears no resemblance to Blackmore's description of it but, after a great deal of searching on the moors, the perfect waterslide, which fitted identically with the story, was found a little way off the main road at Dunkery Gate. It was decided to use this for the filming of John's waterslide entrance into the Doone Valley (whereas the shots of John fishing in Badgeworthy Water were actually filmed in Badgeworthy). However two weeks before filming the waterslide sequence, it was found that the long, hot summer had dried up the waters completely. To overcome this problem the T.V. crew finally 'phoned the Somerset Fire Service who brought a tanker of seawater to the site. This was then poured down the dried bed of the waterslide from the summit whilst the actor playing John Ridd slowly made his way to the top.

They came across many other interesting little problems. One was finding a suitable location for Lorna's Bower. As no such place fitting Blackmore's description exists in the Doone Valley, a little place was finally found which seemed ideal, but before this place could be used a solemn promise had to be given not to make its whereabouts public as nearby grew a rare species of wild orchid, and it was feared that should many people visit this place they might trample all over these orchids, without realizing how precious the flowers were.

Where at all possible the filming was done at Oare, but, as the little notice at Oare Church states, it would have been impossible for Carver Doone to look through the window, and to have shot Lorna at the altar as the church now stands so the T.V. wedding was filmed at the little church at Culbone, and the scene where Carver's gun was pushed through the window, was in actual fact filmed from a reconstruction at the B.B.C. studios in London.

The scenes from the Battle of Sedgemoor were filmed on Sedgemoor itself and that site is certainly worth the visitor's attention. The scene of Tom Faggus's discovery in the farm court-yard was taken on a farm near Porlock.

There are no dangerous bogs on the moors today, Blackmore's account of Cloven Rocks, where Carver Doone met his end, is a figment of the imagination. The filming of this fight and the ensuing death in the bog did cause many complications. For instance, one could not expect any actor to go into a real bog. To overcome this a water tank was sunk into the ground at the location, filled up with slurry mud and covered in peat. Then the actor, very cleverly, to give the impression that he was sinking into the mire, first bent his knees, knelt down and then lowered himself as if he were sinking until finally, taking a deep breath, he submerged completely.

Lorna Doone is such an interesting book that it is certainly worth your while to read it in its original text, for there is a wealth of detail in it which would be impossible to include in any shortened version.